TEMPORALE

MARINA WARNER

Temporale

CENTER FOR WRITERS & TRANSLATORS
THE AMERICAN UNIVERSITY OF PARIS

—

SYLPH EDITIONS

T HE CHILD COULDN'T TELL THE TIME. It was 1953, and she was looking up at the clock hanging on the wall in the vast, shadowy, central rotunda of her new school in Brussels, and couldn't read the hands. Why she'd been asked to leave the classroom and find out the time is unclear; surely the classroom had a clock of its own – perhaps it was broken? That child was sombre and earnest, eager to obey, keen to shine, and determined not to cry as she twisted one of her thin plaits round her fingers and stuck her thumb in her mouth, hoping someone would come and tell her the time so she could give her teacher what she wanted. Above her, the looming vault was entirely painted – a confusion of figures, gloomy and histrionic, soldiers, martyrs, angels in medieval clothes. She felt very small.

I was seven and newly enrolled in the Institut des Dames de Marie, a large Catholic school in a suburb of Brussels called Uccle. My father Esmond was a bookseller – we had come to live in Belgium because, after his bookshop in Cairo was burned down in the uprising of 1952, he had been made manager of the Brussels branch of W. H. Smith. My new school was an ample, imposing, freckled brick pile, Gothic crossed with Art Nouveau, with huge windows and a tall central porch leading onto the Rue Edith Cavell; it was a short drive from the house my father had rented for us. We weren't far from the Grand' Place and central Brussels, on the Avenue de Fré, a long broad suburban street lined with substantial houses standing in herbaceous gardens. Ours had a barn where swallows arrived each summer to nest in the eaves. My father knew about birds, and the swallows made him happy; he built a bird table in the garden and recorded the visitors who came to feed there. A large predator raided one morning: a shrike! The excitement at this shark of the air – rare, handsome, cruel – was intense. The swallows, I was to learn, announced the turning season – timekeepers by instinct.

Telling the time that afternoon was complicated because I was only starting to learn French and even if I could have read the clock, I hadn't yet learned to calculate backwards over the twenty-four hours in the French way, when twenty-to-four is *seize heures moins vingt*. It became a family joke that my younger sister Laura asked, soon after we arrived in Belgium: 'Why won't you tell me in English what *gardener* is in French?' Now and then the

teacher would help me or ask one of my fellow pupils to explain.
I shared a desk with Chantal – the name was new to me – who
was impressively neat and could paint a chequered tile floor in
perfect perspective. When I didn't understand *ananas* or *coccinelle*,
Chantal would draw a *pineapple* for me, or the teacher would
sketch a *ladybird* on the blackboard. (It is miraculous how children
learn a language, whichever it is, Xhosa or Tagalog, no matter
how remote from their mother tongue, how quickly it is absorbed
from playmates and surroundings in schools and on streets;
there is an anecdote from the Princeton Institute of Advanced
Studies, where scholars come from all over the world and send
their offspring to the local kindergarten, that one year, a little boy
from Russia had such a towering personality that, within weeks,
the other children were speaking in Russian, too.) What I did not
yet realise, as I stood baffled by this need to number the passing
hours, is that time is not lived as points on a dial but as pictures in
the mind's eye, and those pictures – *phantasmata* as Aristotle called
them – are woven of experiences in language. Memory translates
numbers into significant stories: the end-of-term, a birthday. A
clock or a watch successfully imposes order on the tumult of
life as it goes by, but *le temps perdu* and *le temps retrouvé* unfold in
words and pictures – Proust's magic lantern slides – not digits.
The words *telling* and *teller* in English reveal how time translates
into narratives, for as well as referring to narrating and speaking,
they are used for counting, as in *telling your beads*, or *bank teller*.
Chronicle contains the word for time, *chronos*; a journal, diary, or
yearbook, all these forms of timekeeping are ways of storytelling,
acts of language.

French entered me through brand names, favourite sweets,
sights and topics overheard in the daily round: *patates*, which
made my father curl his lip in derision at the Belgians' coarseness
(*pommes de terre* was judged more civilised). In those early Brussels
days I discovered: *La Vache Qui Rit*, the fatty cheese with a picture
of a smiling cow; *Au Beau Noir*, printed on the coat hangers from
the laundry – a shadow of colonialism; *vidange*, the refund on the
tall litre bottles of milk; *dentelle*, the lace made by women who
sat in the streets with a cushion in front of them studded with
pins; *dragées*, the sugar almonds given for christenings, pastel-
blue for a boy, pastel-pink for a girl, mixed in with silver and gold;

le Mannequin Pis, the little boy who pees into a fountain off the Grand' Place, mascot of Brussels and another spur to my father's contempt for Belgian taste (whereas I found him fascinatingly naughty and bold). Our house number was *cent nonante*, that *nonante*, like *septante*, Belgian French, a more pragmatic way of counting than the French French *quatre-vingt-dix* and *soixante-dix*. I learned to cross my sevens (and still do). Snow fell that winter in Brussels, my first snow, deep enough to toboggan in the parks. *Luge* was a word I learned when Daddy, yielding to our begging, bought one. Had my southern-Italian mother ever seen snow? Perhaps a dusting of icing sugar on the fields, but never such a heavy duvet. In the playground, we slid over patches of ice to harden and polish them to a slippery shine: *verglas*. *La Butte du Lion*, the steep mound on the battlefield of Waterloo, which we would drive to with visitors from London, where Daddy would stride about, saying, 'The Prussians outflanked the French here... Here x thousand men fell, and the ground is still soaked in their blood... See how the walls are pockmarked with shells.' I would hunt for traces in the ploughed earth, hoping for a splinter of bone or a brass button from a uniform: 1815 felt very close.

Belgium had a twee side – posies, lace collars, lilies of the valley – combined with ribaldry and rudeness recognisable in some Flemish art featuring Fools mooning. My parents complained that Belgium wasn't France. Even when Brussels hosted the World Fair and built the space age Atomium, they longed for Paris, where W. H. Smith has a famous branch on the rue de Rivoli, but whose manager was not moving on, obliging them to make do with Brussels.

At Les Dames de Marie we were given twice-weekly lessons in Flemish – as the language was called at the time, being then considered a dialect of the Dutch spoken in the Netherlands (whereas today, Dutch literature includes the work of Belgian writers). We were all learning French, too, even when it was my classmates' mother tongue: lots of *dictées* and lessons in irregular verbs, which we chanted till we knew them by heart. In history and geography, we repeated lists of dates and facts: at one time, I could recite the products of every Belgian industrial town, and the course of the country's *fleuves* from source to sea. And of

course, we also parroted our times tables. We lined up every
morning in the central assembly hall, and one class at a time
we filed out to our classrooms singing a hymn or a marching
song: '*Malbrouck s'en va-t-en guerre, Miron tomiron tomiron taine...*'
Or, another, which made an even deeper impression on me, the
'*Marche Lorraine*' which contained lines about '*Jeanne la Lorraine*'
and '*ses sabots don daine*'. (I later discovered what *sabots* were, but
have never known exactly what '*don daine*' means. Then as now
I thought that Jeanne d'Arc's shoes were 'neat', in the American
sense. High end of the range clogs. Cool clogs.)

The hymns and marches we enjoyed belting out were training
us, as we all soared to a special high note to cry out:

> *Sur nous plane l'ombre sereine*
> *De Jeanne d'Arc vierge souveraine!*

These were French patriotic songs, but in Belgium less than a
decade after the war, this loyalty was not challenged: Jeanne d'Arc
symbolised resistance to the Nazi occupation of both countries.
She was a heroine and, in contrast to the Virgin Mary and most
other saints, an anomaly, fierce and rebellious. Words and music
together imprinted a language more indelibly than speech: I shall
still be able to quaver '*La Marche Lorraine*' in my eighties. Like
lullabies, the earliest sounds we are likely to hear (if we're lucky),
which communicate the characteristics of a language to the infant
in diphthong or vowel combinations typical of the mother tongue
(which no foreigner can acquire later in life, no matter how fluent
they become), these musical memories may be the last traces
to fade.

I was also praying in French, and this is the side of my educa-
tion that bears most closely on telling the time, on being able to
picture the year turning, to know one day from the next. Daddy
brought me home a missal, bound in pale calf, with a cross, a
triangle, and the Holy Ghost descending, all embossed on the
cover: *Missel quotidien et vespéral*, it says on its spine, and it had
marbled endpapers and gilded fore-edges, over 1,500 pages of
prayers and rites and lists of saints, including an appendix on
Belgian diocesan saints, all of them very obscure. It is a bilingual
missal, French and Latin, because those were the languages of
the Sunday Mass which I attended with my mother and my sister.
(Daddy was an uncommitted Anglican but had kept his promise

made to the priest when he married my devoutly Catholic mother in Bari in 1944, that he would bring up any children in the Catholic faith.) Pope Pius XII was on the throne of St Peter; before Vatican II, an atmosphere of glutinous reverence surrounded the Pope and every priest and nun we encountered, and this piety blended with fascination with royalty, fed by the ups and downs of the Belgian rulers; I was being steeped in monarchism, nationalism, and faith, with a dose of paternalistic colonialism. We prayed for the souls of Congolese babies, and were urged to adopt one of our own as our special care; we were invited to coo over photographs of the Pope in the Vatican gardens, in gleaming spotless white soutane and skullcap, feeding lambs, their fleece an immaculate snowy white. This ethos was compounded by the paintings and stained glass in the school chapel, showing angels and gory martyrdoms, and by the observance of local saints' feast days, such as Ste Gudule, patron saint of Brussels, or Ste Dymphe, who was sexually assaulted by her father and who later became, by one of those knight's moves of Catholic psychology, the patron saint of the mentally disturbed.

Three years later, the missal travelled with me to St Mary's Convent, Ascot, where the services were still in Latin, which meant I wouldn't be left out in spite of my prayerbook being half in French. Daddy wanted me to be taught in England; he was worried his daughter was turning into a foreigner, and I put up no struggle, as I was consuming boarding school adventures by Enid Blyton, Angela Brazil et al. and was keen to join those splendid lacrosse-playing heroines and hold midnight feasts in the dorm. In the event I was terribly homesick, treated as an outsider because my English was formal (I had only spoken it with grownups and the speedy slang of my fellow boarders was entirely foreign to my ears, as they shouted, 'Bags I', 'Fains', and 'Quis? Ego!'). We pupils at St Mary's led the lives of little nuns, and my missal was in daily use; pages have fallen out from the middle where the ordinary of the Mass appears, for every morning we went to hear Mass and take communion. The priests came from a nearby community of Franciscans, and we liked Father Alfred best because he was the youngest and the burliest and – most importantly – the fastest. When we saw him sweep in in his vestments from the sacristy door to the altar steps, and begin, '*Introibo ad altare dei*', we would cheer silently because he could get through the service and communion in twenty minutes. Another of the monks, bent with arthritis and wheezy, would cause us to groan heartlessly when he appeared, furious as we were that our beans on toast would be cooling on the breakfast trolleys while he laboured through the service and crawled from one of us to another at the communion rail. The priest was often assisted by an altar boy from a local village – a *server* – who would vigorously swing a censer and, later, hold a paten under our chins to catch crumbs as they fell from the host. These local lads in their surplices had something over us – we girls were not allowed into the space of the sanctuary near the altar, on the grounds that we were impure.

> *Salve regina, mater misericordiae,*
> *Vita dulcedo et spes nostra salve.*
> *Ad te clamamus exsules filiae Hevae*
> *Ad te suspiramus, gementes et flentes*
> *In hac lacrimarum valle.*

So we sang, again and again, we exiled sinners, groaning and weeping in this vale of tears which we daughters of Eve had brought about.

Every morning, we were woken by a nun entering the dormitory and, later, in the sixth form, coming into our own room, intoning '*Dominus vobiscum*', to which from under the bedclothes we had to murmur, '*Et cum spiritu tuo*', to show we were awake. After Mass, during which it was not uncommon for one of us to faint (we had to fast before taking communion), we went to breakfast where we stood for grace, which was pronounced before and after every meal. At 6 a.m., midday, and 6 p.m., the bells above the chapel rang the Angelus; twice a week, we went to Benediction, the evening ritual with prayers and singing, and on Fridays we made our confessions in the chapel, where one of the friars in a dark box with a starry screen through which only his shadowy form was visible, would hear us – indulgently. We also said the rosary, sometimes in the Lourdes grotto in the crypt underneath the high altar. The statue of Mary as she appeared to Bernadette, the young shepherd girl

from the Pyrenees, stood in a niche among craggy rocks, all made
of cork oak ('from the Holy Land', Mother Emmanuel told us,
in a reverent whisper) festooned with rosaries – beads made of
cut glass, amethyst, or olive wood, which had been dedicated
to Our Lady by others who had come to pray there before us.
Owning a beautiful rosary caused fierce rivalry, but the mother-
of-pearl, olive wood, and crystal beads were expensive, and I
never had enough pocket money for one. I made my own, with
knotted string and wooden beads, and in the dark and cobwebbed
rhododendron bushes that grew abundantly in the grounds of the
convent I built myself my own grotto. I would keep my eyes tight
shut while invoking Our Lady, and then open them suddenly, like
a child playing peekaboo, to catch her before she could disappear.
At 'Holy Shop' (which alternated with 'Sweet Shop') I bought a
plastic Jesus-on-the-cross that glowed; I used to take him to bed
with me and read under the bedclothes by his light.

Sacred languages are not vernaculars, but they are held in common;
they are ancient but calling them *dead* isn't right; they live, in certain
contexts only, such as rituals, many performances of Christian
pieces of music, or sacred dramas. In 1972, in Bali, I was present at
a nightlong *wayang* or puppet performance of the Ramayana in a
coconut grove of a village near Kuta Beach where I was staying; the
dalang chanted the story in Sanskrit and the audience, old and young,
men and women, joined in, knowing the lines by heart. The ear
doesn't baulk at the incomprehensible, but can find it pleasurable,
familiar; the lines can even fit easily to the tongue that does not
fully comprehend them. Language in this form moves closer to
music: a tune you know. This is a state of knowledge that hasn't
been fully explored, as far as I know: understanding a language
without being able to use it as one does one's own, for which one
knows how to combine and recombine its elements.

Latin was like a map which gave me landmarks and orientation,
but I could not use it to go anywhere beyond the boundaries
of the religion I was raised in. There were many other rituals
conducted in French at the convent in Belgium and in English at
St Mary's: the stations of the cross, which we performed during
Lent, processing round the chapel where each scene from the
Passion of Christ was carved in wood on small panels; we were

prompted by Mother Bridget or Sister Louise to imagine as hard as we could the pain Jesus was suffering at every stage of his Via Dolorosa. On the feast of Corpus Domini, the host was carried aloft through the convent grounds and certain girls were picked to be *strewers*: they walked backwards in front of the priest who was holding up the glittering gold monstrance; at every third step, they would curtsey and scatter flower petals from baskets hanging on ribbons from their necks. I was never chosen, to my immense disappointment.

Some of us were studying Latin, but that made no difference to the acceptance of a common currency by others. The phrases did not need to be translated or understood. The word *religion* might derive from *religare*, to bind: we were being bound together by an ancient calendar in an old tongue that none of us understood. In *Crowds and Power*, Elias Canetti points out how the Catholic church, over its millennia-long history, developed methods of unparalleled efficacity in handling large groups; the calendar – the shared keeping of feasts and memorials – is one of them.

Ideologies always have a stake in timekeeping, for radicals and conservatives alike. Augustus Caesar paid particular attention to the cycle of feast days, celebrating many personally in his role as Pontifex Maximus but also inaugurating many more, in this way consolidating his power. At the macro scale, be it in ancient Rome, Christendom, the Muslim world, or communist China, the celebration of feasts and the memorialisation of people and events play a part in governing the people. The ambition to name and control time also dominates, at a more micro scale: heterotopias such as prisons, boot camps, religious cults, holiday camps, factories, alongside boarding schools and monasteries, necessarily impose a structure of time on their inmates and employees.

But this background in social conformism and coercion does not mean the practice cannot be adapted to help distinguish one day from the next more richly, more satisfyingly than what is offered by the arid numerics of the digital clock. Could renewed attention to ways of timekeeping enliven existence? I have come to believe that the language-practices of my childhood faith set firm fundamental principles for my work as a writer: confession encouraged introspection and self-scrutiny; prayers such as the rosary and the stations of the cross stimulated mental image-making and cultivated empathy; the sanctuaries and the processions staged re-enactments which were like dramas, or amateur theatricals. The training I received, to animate cork and stone, plaster and paint with stories, has stood me in good stead, I think. The Lourdes grotto was quiet and secret and mysterious, it had an exciting in-betweenness, the outside brought inside, natural and artificial at the same time, a private spot, akin to a wild animal lair, or a burrow, or a den.

In the 'Ode to Psyche' Keats pledges himself to serve Psyche, whom he evokes as a purely pagan spirit of love, and promises:

A rosy sanctuary will I dress
With the wreath'd trellis of a working brain . . .

Not all writing is bent on building a den or a lair or a refuge, let alone a rosy sanctuary, but at present, when so much violence is happening everywhere and to so many, the desire to create a sanctuary dominates me. And it has let me see something in the rituals of my Catholic childhood that might serve this aim.

A long while ago, I became aware that the religious discipline I underwent had indoctrinated me in Catholic dogma, in the religion's values and morals – and gender expectations. The discourse, the content, the dramatis personae – Mary, Baby Jesus, the angel Gabriel, Joseph, the tortured Virgin Martyrs such as Agatha and Catherine – loomed to fill the canvas of my consciousness and, having filled me with hope and love and yearning to be near them, to be like them, they then stirred in me fury and despair, as I rejected the religion of my girlhood.

At some point a long time ago, I put away that Belgian missal: I hid it behind some books. I didn't want to see its spine on the shelves and remember those days of Catholic fervour.

Yet near the start of the two years and more of the Coronavirus pandemic and the lockdowns, I began thinking about the way time was marked by feasts and holy days, how the dull everyday was translated into stories by the liturgy, and, in a flash, I remembered where I'd stowed my missal, and fished it out unerringly. Did this rediscovery, and my sudden renewed interest in the calendar, mean Catholicism was taking me back? Was I yet another case

of 'once a Catholic'...? But the answer is no – I am inured to the seductions of faith, I still resist a faith grounded in sacrifice, and the message of salvation that the annual religious cycle communicates does not persuade me; yet the practices of faith and their deep structures appear to be a way in which, over centuries of imagination, the wreathed trellis of working brains has built a shelter from chaos, from the shapeless time-space continuum we inhabit. Now I see a structure beneath the doctrines, like a watermark: the liturgical year is a very old way of timekeeping, from an era before watches, before digital clocks. It's a clock set to run for a whole year, like one of those intricate and awe-inspiring orreries that reproduces the interrelated circlings of the solar system.

During the pandemic, the daily rhythm of life in lockdown had a peculiar effect; we all felt it. Days slipped by, undefined, seemingly interchangeable. Another Sunday arrived hard on the heels of the one before. Yet, while time speeded up, it also slowed. It was as if Time weren't wielding a scythe or wheeling about the heavens in a winged chariot but was accosting us – like an accordion player who stretches out the music in an infinity of wheezing, and then suddenly squashes his instrument tight and sticks there, in dumb and threatening silence. The identical days made them feel arrested; yet events that had taken place in 2019 – the last visit to Italy, the last New Year's Eve party – seemed sunk in Jurassic strata of deep time. This monotony was shot through with dread that came and went, and still comes and goes with terrible intensity. Death was closer: for others, for me, as anguish at time disappearing would not be appeased.

Then, gradually, over the long months, I became accustomed to the restrictions, and my experience of time began to change again. The sense of empty days disappeared; there was no longer any moment for tidying drawers or mending a broken chair. Only the fugitive speed remained: each day had gone – puff! – like a cartoon drawing of Bugs Bunny scooting off. The combination of this plague-stricken suspension – the new Covidian temporality – and the dread of worse just over the horizon gave me a new sense of old forms of timekeeping: calendars, with their red-letter days and anniversaries, their high days and holidays and the sacred duet of *temporale* and *sanctorale*, and almanacs, with their reminders of feast days, cycles of the moon and the stars, and corresponding confident prognostications. Did the attachment of each passing day to a different event, miracle, or saint, help mark the endless repetitive flow, in the same way that a buoy out at sea will provide a landmark for sailors in the undifferentiated expanse of open water?

The daily lives of men and women and children enclosed in establishments such as monasteries and foundling hospitals, or living and working on the land, needed these ways of measuring the seasons and the days to know where they were in time and space. Susan Sontag famously quoted: 'Time is necessary so that everything doesn't happen all at once, and space is necessary so that it doesn't all happen to you.' Calendars and almanacs are time-maps, and apart from their survival today as gifts, they are a feature of a pre-digital era, superannuated: GPS knows where you are if you're lost, and you can keep precise atomic time on your i-wear. But calendars and almanacs survive because they are helping to differentiate passing time. Our pre-digital ancestors made schedules and charts to situate themselves, especially in relation to longer arcs of time than the local church bells or the town clock provided. Living in lockdown, in conditions which brought us together across the globe, I began to search timekeeping strategies in the past, even in those heterotopias – monasteries, prisons, boarding schools. In spite of the disciplinary intentions, could such methods be recuperated for better purposes? Did folk narratives, pious and not so pious, plot coordinates to prevent the sameness, this double sense of time on a loop as well as jammed and imploding? Attaching a strange and wonderful story to each day, just as Boccaccio's bubble of narrators does in *The Decameron*, seems an ingenious use of imagination to lift the depression and tedium of enforced shielding from plague.

Picking up my missal and feeling it again, the squishiness of the binding (it is coming apart and there is foam backing under the leather) brought me up against that Belgian child I used to be. Gradually, over the months of sequestered existence at a single address, my similar secluded existence came vividly back to me, those years at my convent schools in the late fifties and early sixties. In Uccle, Belgium, from 1953 to 1956, and later in Ascot, Berkshire, from the autumn of 1956 to 1963, I was held in an unfolding drama and, within that overarching story, connected to

a huge cast of people and their stories that were partly contained in that missal, stories often bizarre, bloody, human. These were the lives of the saints, one of whom was remembered each day in that morning Mass. Sometimes they came in pairs (Peter and Paul, Cosmas and Damian) or even in very large groups (St Ursula and her 11,000 Virgins, all massacred together). Specific prayers followed from their status as Confessors or Martyrs or Virgin Martyrs, and the priest's robes when he came in to say Mass would give us a clue as to which office in the missal to use to follow the service.

Sumptuous Books of Hours made in the Middle Ages and Renaissance recorded these feast days and saints' days, weaving them into the unfolding agricultural year, with illuminations of monthly tasks, weather, harvests. Many such manuscripts are matchless and precious artifacts made for princes, such as the *Très Riches Heures du Duc de Berri* or the *Hours of Anne of Cleves*, in which saints appear with their emblems (St Gertrude, who protects those who suffer from a phobia for mice, appears with rats and mice chasing around her; St Laurence, patron saint of chefs, carries the griddle on which he was roasted to death), richly surrounded by decorative borders and, in the lower margin, comic and grotesque doodles. Did these glorious polychrome pages provide ways of overcoming the daily tedium? Only the rich could acquire these remedies against monotony, but the stories that inspired the illuminations weren't behind a paywall. They were evoked in the daily Mass, helping to distinguish one day from the next, and would be picked up in sermons and pictures and gossip: the nuns at my school relished relating scenes of assault and vindication. In 1902, Maria Goretti (feast day, 6 July), was eleven years old when she was killed by a neighbour who had attempted to rape her; in 1950, she was canonised in the presence of her mother and her murderer. She was a favourite subject of our bedtime stories.

It used to puzzle me that *The Golden Legend*, the massive 14th-century repertory of extreme martyrdoms and incredible wonders, along with later, magisterial volumes such as Butler's *Lives of the Saints,* should be organised according to their subjects' feast days. But in fact, the books are primarily calendars. We tend to think of such stories as evidence of religious beliefs and rituals, but, as Walter Benjamin points out in his essay 'The Storyteller', storytelling flourishes when men and women are imprisoned in repetitive tasks, shelling peas, preserving fruit, fulling cloth. 'Boredom,' he writes, 'is the dream bird that hatches the egg of experience.' As the nightmarish twists and turns of the virus filled the news with information that felt futile, different stories, outlandish, impossible, unverifiable, became a way of overcoming terminal ennui.

In the past I have denounced the salaciousness of such stories of saints, their sadomasochism, and their advocacy of victimhood as the grounds of ethics for women. The material, I now see, is close to popular entertainment: horror, crime fiction, even pornography. Hagiography is a narrative genre, a mix of report, gossip, anecdote, political claims, and flights of fancy; it draws on the great granary of popular narrative imagination and sets it into the very structure of daily existence. It's not usually considered alongside fiction because it's sacred literature: for believers, the stories have a special kind of authority, not exactly scriptural, but close. For non-believers the tales have another kind of value. Aside from questions of historical veracity, the stories that fill the liturgical calendar are weird and startling; they speak truthfully in the same way that a fable such as Franz Kafka's *Metamorphosis* does (and Kafka was inspired by local and Yiddish folklore). The freak-show qualities of some hagiography make it surprising that the depicted figures should be considered holy, but if you switch from theological expectations to look at their adventures as a desperate remedy for the drudgery, dreariness, and sheer misery of the daily grind, they become a kind of popular fiction, an offshoot of the fantastic. Arabic has a term for the literature of wonder – *'ajā'ib*, which contrasts with the term *adab*, a category closer to *belles lettres*. Critics tend not to have thought of hagiography as a branch of literary fantasy, since it is written as true history and expects to be believed, whereas fantastic literature invokes a supernatural that is undecided and indeterminate, not divine truth. In contemporary culture, these boundaries are yielding.

The message of salvation that the annual religious cycle communicates does not persuade me, yet the method of enlivening each day, of marking off the passage of time, strikes me as a way ahead.

The cycle of *temporale*, the sequence of the offices or rituals for the moveable feasts, was braided into the cycle of *sanctorale*, the feasts kept on certain days, year in year out. The holiest days were picked out in scarlet by medieval scribes in their Books of Hours and liturgical calendars: red-letter days. *Temporale* gave out a changing rhythm: Easter, Whitsun, and it included special single events to celebrate – Good Friday, Easter Sunday. Together with *sanctorale*, the cycle of fixed feasts such as the Annunciation, All Saints, and Christmas, and all individual saints' days, this calendar is mapped onto the old pagan festivals, just as state holidays in many countries now take place on days that were once sacred: 1 May, the closing day of the Floralia in Imperial Rome in honour of the goddess Flora, became the feast of Labour and was later translated by the Vatican into the feast of St Joseph the Worker.

This sequence is above all a series of stories, arranged into a mnemonic pattern. It may be thought of in terms of prosody, how scansion and rhyme add point to a poem, how memory can take the print of the lines more readily than a similar thought written in prose and lift a commonplace to the stars. ('Thus have I had thee as a dream doth flatter, / In sleep a king but waking no such matter.' 'Wild nights – Wild nights! / Were I with thee / Wild nights / Should be our luxury!')

The liturgy acts analogously to metre and rhyme, adding personality to the quotidian: if Mondays still have a certain feel, and Fridays likewise, due to the rhythm of an ordinary week (in the Western world), then the Mass we attended every morning as children and the songs we sang there added a particular flavour to that Monday, to that Friday, because when Father Alfred strode into the sanctuary in his sturdy old sandals under his silk and satin – red vestments meant a martyr, white a confessor (the celebrant might even be arrayed in rose, very occasionally, for specially joyful days) – we'd have to hunt at the back of our missals where the calendar listed lesser-known saints to find the right readings from the gospels for that day. The search was like a pinch, it could give a twist of interest to that morning. Ah yes, St Astius! Smeared with honey and stung to death by wasps to punish him for refusing to abjure Christianity.

A story from today's date, 26 April (a red-letter day for me because I gave birth to my son on this day): SS Cletus and

Marcellinus, two early successors to St Peter, who like him were martyred in Rome (one of whom gave his name to a vast catacomb in the periphery of the city). This information would be enough for us girls to imagine the heroic struggles of early Christians thrown to the lions, the crowd baying, giving the thumbs down. Persecution was somehow affirmative, thrilling. The mention of martyrs lit up the cinema in the brain (we were allowed to watch spectaculars such as *Quo Vadis*).

Almost any day will yield anecdotes and memories – wonder tales. St Christina the Astonishing (died 1150, feast day 24 July) rose from her coffin high into the air and lived on, performing feats that earned her her sobriquet. St Joseph of Cupertino also flew, in view of many witnesses and on numerous occasions – and he lived in modern times (he died in 1663, feast day 18 September). St Apollonia (feast day 9 February) can be identified from the pair of pincers she carries, in memory of her torments: she had all her teeth pulled out and is therefore the patron saint of dentists. St Christopher sometimes appears with a dog's head like a victim of Circe's enchantments, but in 1961 his authenticity was doubted, and he was expunged from the ranks of the saints as part of a major cull. (I remember how Sister Philomena cried when she was helping me at bathtime, because her patron saint had been declared an archaeological error: an inscription on a sarcophagus in the catacombs had been read as a proper name, when it was probably a routine blessing; Philomena the child martyr, the patroness of babies, had become a figment and the old Irish nun who cherished her was bereft.) The tenth-century English saint, Edith (died 984, feast day 16 September), grew up in the abbey of Wilton with her mother, Wulfthryth, who had been abducted from Wilton by her husband, Edith's father, King Edgar the Peaceful. He did penance for his sin thereafter, while Wulfthryth returned to the nunnery and became its abbess, taking the child of her rape, Edith, with her. Mother and daughter loved fine clothes and their community was dressed in gold and white robes, in the same high style which another towering personality, St Hildegard of Bingen, liked her flock and choir to enjoy in her abbey at Rupertsberg.

The marking of time does not need to conform to a religion or a religious calendar or to an ideology commanding allegiance, not least as this would lead to even more interfaith tensions than are raging already in our conflicted world. Some new adherence to the breviary is not what I am thinking of – far from it. Nor should any more days be added to the current commercial opportunities, when Valentine's Day, Mother's and Father's Days, as well as Halloween, are being exploited for tawdry ends and shopping bonanzas – Prime Day at Amazon, Black Friday before Xmas. But something richer and more personal could be built, closer to the keeping of birthdays and anniversaries, entangled with personal memories and connections. An example would be the name days that Slavic peoples and Greeks respect, linked in turn to the Orthodox calendar of feast days. My own saint, Marina, lived disguised as a boy – the monk Marinus – and was accused of fathering a child. She accepted the blame in silence and is counted as one of the earliest fluidly gendered figures in history. Her miraculously preserved body is on display, a tiny, whitened cadaver, in Santa Maria Formosa in Venice.

In some ways, these old ways of timekeeping evolved into the daily paper, news feeds, and Instagram posts – different every day, and even every moment of the day, following vivid human stories and exciting often wild and emotional responses in the reader/ user. But the news is a narrative form predicated on past events or taking place as the day unfolds, and it is presumed to connect to truth-telling, to reportage and witness. The genres collected in the annual religious calendar – and even more so in less pious almanacs – are wonder tales, miracles, and mysteries. Their truth-telling has a mystical and symbolic character. Their narrative mode lies closer to poetry and fable than to journalism. They do not lay a strong claim to documentary verity, unlike a newspaper or social media stream (no matter how fraudulent). They occupy the territory of the fantastic, and our forebears distinguished these stories from historical records.

While still at work on the *Metamorphoses*, Ovid, supreme storyteller, began another long narrative poem, the *Fasti* (*Feasts*), a calendar poem that ranges far beyond the seasons and the weather; the poet embroiders origin stories about local Roman cults and holidays, the particular deities they celebrated, and the histories they were based on. He only managed to cover six months – January to June – before he died, but he was clearly enjoying himself as he gave free rein there to his prodigious narrative powers, his wit, his mischievousness, his knowledge. In his *Metamorphoses*, Ovid translates landscape into myth: springs, mountains, cliffs, whirlpools, reefs, sulphurous vents, these all attract his mythmaking; he reprises episodes from the *Odyssey* and other predecessors but adds richly to these. In the *Fasti*, he reads the days of the turning seasons in a similar way, taking off from their names and the supposed facts they recall and riffing fantastically: he imagines Dido's sister Anna washing up shipwrecked on a beach near Rome where Aeneas comes upon her and recognises and welcomes her, deliriously delighted to see her again. Ovid then identifies this Anna, from the simple identity of their names, with the popular local divinity Anna Perenna, who was worshipped at her shrine in Rome, especially by women unlucky in love or suffering other woes – a site that recently yielded a hoard of votive tablets, inscribed with entreaties, curses, and spells.

Could Ovid's lead be followed, and his way of combining inherited beliefs with original ideas become a model for inspiration? All over the English-speaking world, long abandoned gods and goddesses, from an eclectic array of pantheons, still lend their names to the days of the week: Monday for the moon, Tuesday for the god Tui (identified with Mars, as in *mardi* or *martedi*, French and Italian for Tuesday), Friday for Freya from Norse mythology, Saturday after Saturn the Roman god, and Sunday for the Greek god Apollo (while in many European languages this is the Lord's Day, *dimanche, domenica*). But these words are dead metaphors, they no longer trail the stories that first defined them.

In a poem from her recent collection, *Lurex*, Denise Riley evokes the saints and martyrs she also knows, their stories and emblems. She closes with a question that is also a wish:

What hope is there of a purely secular grace?

And segues into an epiphany:

> *Attend, Agnes; your white emblem's bleating.*

With this allusion to the Virgin Martyr Agnes and her lamb, Riley brings the stillness of the image to new life. But the question, '*What hope is there of a purely secular grace?*', goes beyond reawakening dead symbols, beyond giving a conventional sign the animate reality of a bleating animal. Riley sounds sceptical, even despairing, that the secular sphere could ever be infused with grace.

There have of course been attempts made to reawaken the meaningfulness of everyday, some of them tongue-in-cheek, others in earnest. In France in 1793, the French government embarked on reinvigorating Time by inaugurating the Revolutionary Calendar. The undertaking represented a move analogous to adopting the metre as the fundamental unit of measurement; the power to determine such measures was considered divine, and an attribute of supreme authority on earth, symbolised by the rod or tally stick carried by deities in Sumer, Ancient Egypt, and Persia. The Republican week – ten days long – measured time metrically: time under the new regime was to be orderly, classical, centralised – and above all, metric.

This was also a gloriously extravagant and literary undertaking. Ten-day weeks (*décades*) in groups of three in each of the twelve months formed the main structure, leaving five days over for designated special feasts. A *Fête de la Révolution* was to be held every leap year. Philippe-François-Nazaire Fabre, actor, poet, and playwright, was appointed *rapporteur* to the committee charged with devising the new Calendar. Flamboyant and improvident, Fabre had done time in a debtors' prison but had emerged, in 1793, as one of Danton's right-hand men. He had added *d'Églantine*, the French word for honeysuckle, to his very ordinary surname, after he took part in the annual *Jeux Floraux* in Toulouse, a joust in which poets competed with one another. His sonnet to the Virgin Mary, the set topic, did not win, but it is a sign of his panache that, thinking he should have won, he adopted a spray of honeysuckle as his emblem and had himself portrayed carrying a silver replica of the flower. The poet André Chénier and the artist Jacques-Louis David also contributed to the plans for the new regime's timekeeping. They decided the months were to be called after French weather: the year began on 22 September with *Vendémiaire*, after a word for the grape harvest; *Brumaire*, foggy, followed, then *Frimaire*, frosty, then *Nivôse* from Latin for snowy; January was renamed *Pluviôse*, rainy, followed by *Ventôse*, windy;

spring began with *Germinal*, followed by *Floréal*, and *Prairial*; summer included *Messidor* (from another word for harvest), and *Thermidor* from the Greek for heat and gift combined. The close of the republican year, corresponding to August, was called *Fructidor*.

The cycle is a recognisable work of European Romanticism, reverberating with the nature poetry being composed in England at the time by Samuel Taylor Coleridge, William Wordsworth (themselves caught up in revolutionary fervour) and John Clare; but it also, as with so many aspects of the French Revolution, invokes the older exemplary Roman Republic, and echoes the Odes of Horace and the Georgics of Virgil.

Fabre d'Églantine and his colleagues took their task into every corner of French bucolic life. They gave each day its own name, after the country's flora and fauna, its raw materials and crafts and trades. In this way the revolutionaries were following the tradition exemplified by the *Très Riches Heures du Duc de Berri* and the sumptuous Zodiac frescoes of Francesco del Cossa and others in the Palazzo Schifanoia in Ferrara, with their joyously observed pictorial scenes and symbols for each ten-day segment (a *decan* in astrological parlance), and each month's characteristic weather, labours, and pastimes. The Republicans' focus is resolutely pure and incorruptible. No deities, not even Reason or Liberty. No saints. No great men or women. No historical characters, politicians, soldiers, philosophers, poets, artists, past or present. The approach moves from allegory (*Fête de la Vertu, du Génie, de l'Opinion*, etc.) to the phenomenological, generating an encyclopaedic paean to the agriculturalists, traders, and craftworkers of the nation.

The first day of each *décade* is named after a flower, fruit, crop, herb, or substance found at that time of year; accordingly, the spring opens with *Germinal* and the primrose, whereas the winter lists fuel and other raw materials – peat, coal, bitumen, sulphur, saltpetre, granite, marl, lime, gypsum... The fifth and the fifteenth days are named after a domestic or wild animal found throughout *la France profonde* (not forgetting fish and fisherfolk); the tenth and the twentieth days invoke gear and tackle and tools. The range is eccentric and the effect festive, successfully celebrating the ideals of the Revolution while dignifying the lives of the workers. The Calendar does not lift its sights beyond the nation and omits

allusion to any other region – in spite of the vital role the French Caribbean and other colonial possessions played during the turmoil of the Revolution and the rise of Napoleon.

The original Calendar reads like an exuberant list-poem in the Oulipian tradition, somewhat akin to the Walrus's talk '*Of shoes – and ships – and sealing wax – Of cabbages – and kings –*'. It also presents a tough vocabulary test: *Chanvre* (hemp) on 21 *Vendémiaire*; *Fragon* (thorny myrtle) on 3 *Pluviôse*; *Salicorne* (samphire) on 11 *Thermidor*. It reminds me of the children's illustrated dictionary that helped me learn French, which showed scenes of daily life – shopping streets, open markets, garage forecourts, farmyards, harbours, with every item labelled.

The poet Zoë Skoulding, inspired by the French Republican example, has responded in a sustained cycle of poems intended to revivify local lore and knowledge of her own rural Wales; she addresses flowers and fruits, trees and shrubs, tools and gear, includes broccoli and lichen, couch grass and woad, sowbread and celandine, a cow and a hare, a billhook and a dibber. In some of her poems, she has tracked down the English translations of truly abstruse items from the original Calendar: she evokes *Doronic* (for 17 *Ventôse*) as Leopard's Bane:

> Daisy wheel of sun on bitter grey
> where there's no stopping
> on the yellow lines or anywhere –
> leaves furl out to their margins
> irregular and toothed.

Fabre d'Églantine went to the scaffold the year after his Revolutionary Calendar was adopted, alongside his friend Danton, on 5 April 1794 = 16 *Germinal, Laitue* (lettuce). Chénier was beheaded, too, on 25 July 1794 = 7 *Thermidor, Armoise* (mugwort). The system they had devised lasted another ten years, but in 1805, during the Directoire, Napoleon announced a return to Gregorian timekeeping – every day having a different name was unworkable. The Commune reintroduced the Calendar in 1871, but the attempt lasted only 17 days.

A retort was issued in the 1880s, when the pataphysicians began dreaming up an alternative, absurdist calendar; a final version was adopted in 1949, the year after the death of their founder Alfred Jarry. It consisted of thirteen months, each 29 days long, the 29th day being imaginary (with one, or sometimes two exceptions) and a Friday 13th recurring every month. A high-spirited, comic, profane parody, it mocks Christianity's sacred cycle as well as state pietas. The months are given loopy, idiosyncratic names, some of them after private obsessions of Jarry's, adding a particular personality and narrative wit to the compilation. Where Fabre was patriotic and edifying, Jarry's colleagues larked about and blasphemed. One month (6 October to 2 November) is called *Haha*; another (29 December to 25 January) *Décervelage* (*Disembraining*); 18 May to 14 June becomes *Merdre* (translated as *Pshit*), and 11 August to 7 September *Phalle* (*Phallus*). Jarry's love of cycling is remembered in the month of *Pédale* (22 February to 22 March). A fundamental principle of pataphysics, the zany, Dada-esque stance towards life defined by Jarry as 'the science of imaginary solutions', is enshrined in the name of the month from 23 March to 19 April: *Clinamen* (the *Swerve*).

Drawing up a new calendar to suit a community still preoccupies agencies such as the United Nations. Today, in the refugee camps the UN runs, children and families observe a packed sequence of special days to commemorate struggles against illnesses (World Malaria Day) or to encourage various behaviours (World Handwashing Day). This calendar carefully avoids all religious or national references. It is regimenting but earnestly hopeful and inclusive (World Autism Awareness Day; International Mother Earth Day; International Birdsong Day). It aims at global acceptance, to be unifying and eirenic. But it lacks the grain of the storyteller's voice and the flavour of a place and the fun of stories, of fable, fantasy, individual memory, and inherited wisdom. Beyond the NGOs, campaigns for memorial days, as for monuments, keep forming, some with great success: Pride month, for example.

Almanacs, one of the oldest forms of the printed book, were often printed for a certain region and registered local needs, cults, and interests. An almanac is an offshoot of a Book of Hours but tilts its vision away from repetition of past cycles towards future prospects, weather-forecasting and prophecy, horoscopes, recommended times for sowing and harvesting: almanacs entail prognostication. This is a crucial distinction between almanacs and religious calendars: almanacs are generally prospective, looking forward not back, forewarning rather than recording, imagining what might lie ahead in the year to come in order to give the impression that it is possible to be prepared for every eventuality. Almanacs are not bound by faith to any institution, so the stories they contain can be even more fantastic than hagiography. Their contents are essentially heterogeneous as to beliefs, traditionally packed with astrology, medical nostrums, charms and remedies, portents and warnings – in sum, folklore ('superstition'). When print made possible the wide distribution of almanacs, these became a dominant element of early commercial literature, typically carrying notices of fixtures such as auctions, fairs, livestock sales, suppliers, trades notices, and small ads. Later, sports news becomes a major element. They are the recognisable forebears of the news and – to some degree – social media. Their supernatural is not official religion but magic and divination, signs and wonders:

an almanac predicts eclipses of the moon, the transit of Venus, meteor showers, and other less ascertainable phenomena. They serve the locality in which they circulate and are alert to place and its particularities. This makes an almanac more personal than a regular calendar, and open to invention and customisation with added stories. It makes it a more sympathetic model – to each their own almanac!

In 1911, the radical group of artists, writers, musicians, dancers, and thinkers who called themselves *Der Blaue Reiter* (*The Blue Rider*) proclaimed their aesthetic vision: 'Well, I have a new idea…' wrote Wassily Kandinsky, 'A kind of almanac (yearbook) with reproductions and articles…and a *chronicle*!…the entire year must be reflected; and a link to the past as well as a ray to the future must give this mirror its full life.' The artist Franz Marc became Kandinsky's enthusiastic co-editor as they embarked on gathering visionary, provocative pieces by like-minded dreamers – in literature and music as well as the visual arts. August Macke, Arnold Schoenberg, and Paul Klee contributed, using the almanac as a platform for manifestos of their hopes and ambitions. Their interests ranged widely and abolished aesthetic hierarchies: they laid a strong emphasis on vernacular culture – ancient Egyptian shadow puppets, Alaskan weaving, Russian folk art, glass paintings of saints and heroes from Bavaria, children's drawings. Performance, storytelling, the fantastic, the ghostly, the supernatural, were never far from their minds. But the crucial aspect of their work is that their almanac – an eclectic display of artifacts, a call to cultural engagement, and a salmagundi of ideas, beliefs, and references – was making them into a community, or, even, a movement. Compiling it, they joined friends, allies, comrades, and this fostered the intensity and productivity of their vision.

The relation between timekeeping and storytelling corresponds to the celebrated axiom of the Polish-American philosopher, Alfred Korzybski: 'The map is not the territory'. By analogy: the clock is not the day; the timekeeper is not the night. Korzybski meant that the accurate survey of a place does not convey the ways that place is experienced by the inhabitants who live there or travellers who pass through it, and that individual mental orientation charts a place according to many other factors besides the measurements of gradients and distances. Writers have frequently created characters and habitats, which, though they remain invented, are then written back into the fabric, when invention eclipses reality: today, the city of Oxford presents itself as the place of *Alice in Wonderland* and *Harry Potter* (the films were set there). Inventions overlay reality and reality gives way. As Borges writes in 'Tlön Uqbar Orbis Tertius': the truth is, reality wants to give way.

Can something similar be undertaken regarding time as we are living it now? Like the Chinese, we could adopt a guardian animal for each year, not necessarily following the signs of the Zodiac, instead of the dry numbering we use now. With the rise and fall of empires and globalisation, many distinctive calendars have disappeared from use: the Mayans'; the indigenous peoples' of north America and the Pacific. The Ukrainians still have different names for the months: April is the month of Blossom, September, the month of Heather. In a new calendar, the old gods could be remembered haunting the new days; perhaps Friday, that used to belong to Venus and Freya, could allude to love, passion, affairs of the heart. I don't keep anniversaries, and Valentine's Day and Mother's Day upset me because they seem only to cause disappointment. Better to forget my birthday than hope someone else will remember it – though as it happens, I've never succeeded in forgetting it. But, just as celebrating gives us all a chance, when we grow older, to overlook the gloom that another year gone can cast, embroidering time passing might oppose not only tedium but also despair. I like to imagine that presiding genii of the months could be natural wonders, dolphins, sea sponges, starfish, stones, meteors; that certain days could be protected by inspiring musicians and singers, actors and writers and artists; that yet others could be watched over by figures embodying states of feeling, including awkwardness, embarrassment, remorse, anguish, and another by dreamers and inventors; yet others could draw on roaming faraway places. There is no end, really, of ways of enriching the daily round.

Certain dates still mean something to me, sealed into my sense of time from those stories and picture-memories of my childhood: 6 December, *la fête de Saint Nicolas*, was kept in Belgium with more excitement and far more treats and sweets than Christmas itself. Bakers and pâtissiers and confectioners displayed trays upon trays of delicious vividly dyed replica fruits, strawberries, plums, bananas, oranges, pineapples, all made of *pâte d'amandes*, or *massepain*. *Pain d'épices* – a kind of scented gingerbread – was also on offer. But the date meant so much to me because San Nicola is the patron saint of my mother's hometown, Bari. His body was brought there by 77 intrepid sailors who liberated this most precious of relics from the infidels then in power in Myra, in present-day Turkey. There San Nicola – who was to become Father Christmas – had left dowries overnight in the bedroom of three poor dowerless girls and, flying down over the storm-tossed waves, rescued the drowning from a foundering ship. In my mother's southern part of the world, Christmas was subdued by comparison with San Nicola or with La Befana, 6 January, the feast of the three kings. This feast – Epiphany (*la fête des Rois*) – was celebrated in Brussels with a special *galette* in which a bean was hidden: if you found the bean in your helping, the gold-leaf paper crown from around the cake would be yours, queen for the day. La Befana, a name that derives from 'epiphany', has become a real personage in southern Italian folklore: an old woman who failed to give the kings the right information when they asked about the wonderful new-born baby, and so was identified as a witch. Over time, the vagaries of folklore have merged her with San Nicola: she brings good children sweets on the eve of 6 January and bad children a stick or a lump of coal, and in books of fireside tales and legends, she figures as the legendary crone storyteller, another Mother Goose.

But calendar stories don't have to be uplifting or jolly; they can also tell of old unhappy far-off things. They can pierce the *punctum* in memory (as Roland Barthes describes the element in a photograph that makes it speak to him, a detail which can turn something nondescript meaningful). For me, May Day is mixed up with the scent of lilies of the valley: it was the custom in Belgium to exchange posies of *muguets* on that day. They were hawked on the streets at exorbitant prices and with their small white frilled bells and ecstatic scent, they were irresistible and we – my mother, my sister, and I – all wanted some. My father always fretted bitterly about money, and our nagging for a bunch of lilies of the valley set him off into one of his sudden terrifying rages. He was driving us to church when he began to bellow, then drove us straight at a cherry tree in full blossom, stopping just before he hit the trunk, my mother shaking and sobbing in the front seat. He was the breadwinner, so I suppose it wasn't altogether inexplicable that he felt we didn't understand and wished to squander his efforts on silly luxuries. But over the years his temper alienated my mother's love and ours. That was a tragedy for him, too...

One date I always notice when it comes round is 22 November, Saint Cecilia's feast. She is the patron saint of music, martyred in ancient Rome, who appears among the company of heaven playing her psaltery, sitting on a cloud. Much of the music we sang in the choir at school was composed by our Reverend Mother, Mother Cecilia, the heiress of the department store Marshall & Snelgrove, who had brought her immense fortune as a dowry to the convent when she took the veil. She died one term, when I was ten or eleven, and we were all taken to see her on her bier, white flowers piled around her, her face pale, her eyes closed, her white hands threaded with a rosary.

I do not remember what the beads were made of, but certainly something precious. On Saint Cecilia's day there rises inside me again the awe and horror I felt at my first sight of death.

COLOPHON

THE CAHIERS SERIES · NUMBER 39
ISBN: 978-1-909631-43-4

Series Editor: Dan Gunn
Associate Series Editor: Daniel Medin
Design: SYLPH EDITIONS DESIGN
Set in Giovanni Mardersteig's Monotype Dante

Text: © Marina Warner, 2022
Images: © Dimitris Kleanthis, 2022

With thanks to the San Francisco Foundation
for its generous support.

SYLPH
EDITIONS

Published by Sylph Editions, London and
the American University of Paris | 2022

www.sylpheditions.com   www.aup.edu